COULD YOU EVER

WADDLE WITH PENGUINS!?

Written by
Sandra Markle

Illustrated by
Vanessa Morales

Scholastic Inc.

For Karen Berry
and all the children
at Hedgcoxe
Elementary School
in Plano, Texas.

Acknowledgments: The author would like to thank Dr. David Ainley, senior ecologist with H. T. Harvey & Associates, ecological consultants in Los Gatos, California, for sharing his enthusiasm and expertise.

A special thank-you to Skip Jeffery for his loving support during the creative process.

Photos ©: 1, 30: Patrick J. Endres/Getty Images; 4: Jason Edwards/Getty Images; 6, 32: Michael Nolan/Getty Images; 8 and back cover: Nick Dale/Design Pics/Getty Images; 10: Nature Picture Library/Alamy Stock Photo; 12: Gerald Corsi/Getty Images; 14: agefotostock/Alamy Stock Photo; 16: DurkTalsma/Getty Images; 18: KeithSzafranski/Getty Images; 20: Paul Souders/Getty Images; 22 and back cover: Andrew Peacock/Getty Images; 24 and back cover: Fuse/Getty Images; 26: KEVIN ELSBY/Alamy Stock Photo; 31 top and bottom: Imagery from the NASA MODIS instrument, courtesy NASA NSIDC DAAC.

Library of Congress Cataloging-in-Publication Data available

ISBN 978-1-338-85878-5

10 9 8 7 6 5 4 3 2 1   23 24 25 26 27

Printed in the U.S.A.   40
First edition, November 2023

Book design by Maria Lilja

What if one day when you woke up, you weren't quite yourself? What if your whole world had changed? What if you were in Antarctica living with ADÉLIE PENGUINS!?

Adélie penguins are built to stay warm. Stiff outer feathers block out cold. Under those, fluffier feathers trap body heat. So does blubber, the thick fat under their skin. When on land, Adélies fluff up their feathers and hunch down for extra protection against freezing conditions.

When you live with penguins, you will stay toasty warm even during a blizzard.

FACT

An Adélie penguin's outer feathers are tightly packed and overlap like shingles on a roof.

Adélie penguins are birds that fly through the ocean. Their wings are paddlelike flippers that power them forward. Their torpedo-shaped bodies easily slip through the water. And quick leaps into the air let them take breaths without pausing.

When you live with penguins, you will swim races between frozen places.

FACT

Adélie penguins swim as fast as 9 miles per hour to catch food or escape danger.

Adélie penguins dine in the ocean. To eat their fill, they gulp at least 200 mouthfuls of fish, squid, jellyfish, and shrimplike krill a day.

When you live with penguins, you will dive in for breakfast, lunch, and dinner!

FACT

Adélie penguins eat about 4 pounds of seafood a day, if they can catch it.

For a high-energy meal, Adélie penguins catch Antarctic silverfish. But those fish live in the ocean depths. So, to catch one, an Adélie takes a deep breath and, flapping fast, dives down. Down. DOWN! Adélie penguins dive as deep as 590 feet to catch a silverfish.

When you live with penguins, you will hold your breath long enough to view creatures deep down in the Antarctic Ocean.

FACT

Adélie penguins can hold their breath for up to 6 minutes.

Adélie penguins are predators. But they are also prey for leopard seals and orcas. If threatened, Adélies swim fast to the closest place to get out of the water. Then they paddle upward so quickly they fly to a safe landing. It's how Adélie penguins stay out of reach and off the menu.

When you live with penguins, you will perform high jumps. No problem!

FACT

Adélie penguins can leap 6 feet into the air.

Leopard seals seeking dinner hang around land where Adélie penguins gather. So, Adélies never enter the ocean alone. Instead, they pack together until one jumps—or is pushed in. Then the other penguins follow—FAST!

When you live with penguins, you will always let others dive in first.

FACT

Adélie penguins stick together to have help watching out for predators.

During October, in Antarctica's springtime, Adélie penguins head to rocky coastlines. Thousands gather in the same places every year. Those groups become Adélie summer colonies. Once there, many penguins choose mates. Or mates from past years call out to find each other again.

When you live with penguins, you will spend every summer at "The Colony."

FACT

Some Adélie colonies number more than a million penguins.

Adélie penguins scratch out bowl-shaped nests and line them with pebbles. The pebble layer keeps their eggs above any melting snow. But pebbles are rare on rocky Antarctic beaches. And they are so prized, Adélie pairs regularly gift pebbles to each other.

When you live with penguins, you will gift pebbles to your best friends.

FACT

Adélie penguins sometimes sneak pebbles from a neighbor's nest.

All adult Adélie penguins look alike and talk with squawks and brays. But no two penguin voices sound the same. It's how adult mates find each other. Each fluffy, gray chick peeps differently, too. So, parents find and feed their babies among the many chicks in the colony's nursery.

SQUAWK, SQUAWK!

When you live with penguins, every penguin will know your squawk.

FACT

Hungry Adélie chicks call nonstop until a parent finds them and feeds them.

Adélie penguins are built for speedy swimming. Their legs are so short and their feet are so big that when they walk on land they waddle. They also must hop to cross ice gaps or cracks. But Adélies can keep waddle-hopping for miles if they need to.

When you live with penguins, your happy dance will be the waddle-hop.

FACT

Adélie penguins can waddle as fast as 2 miles per hour.

When crossing snow or ice, Adélie penguins often flop on their bellies and toboggan. Rowing with their flippers and kicking with their feet sends them skimming. This is faster than walking, and there is no risk of falling down!

When you live with penguins, you won't need a sled to toboggan like a champion.

FACT

Tobogganing down steep slopes, Adélie penguins go faster than most humans can run.

Adélie penguins sleep on land or during pauses while swimming. But they only ever sleep for a few minutes at a time. These power naps let them rest up while staying alert for any sneaky predator.

When you live with penguins, your bedtime will only last a few minutes.

FACT

When on land, Adélie penguins often sleep standing up because stretching out on ice-cold ground is too chilly.

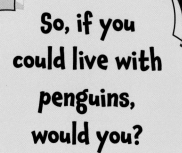

Luckily, you don't have to choose. You will always be who you are and live where people live.

WHERE DO ADÉLIE PENGUINS LIVE?

Adélie penguins live around Antarctica. While Antarctica's winter is freezing and dark, Adélies swim north in small groups. They feed as they travel beyond the ice shelf and jump out to rest on sheets of floating ice.

Like riding a merry-go-round, the ocean's currents carry the penguins in a giant circle. Come October, as Antarctica warms and brightens, they arrive back where they started. Then the Adélies head to their colonies to hatch and raise their chicks.

Some Adélie penguins travel more than 10,000 miles a year!

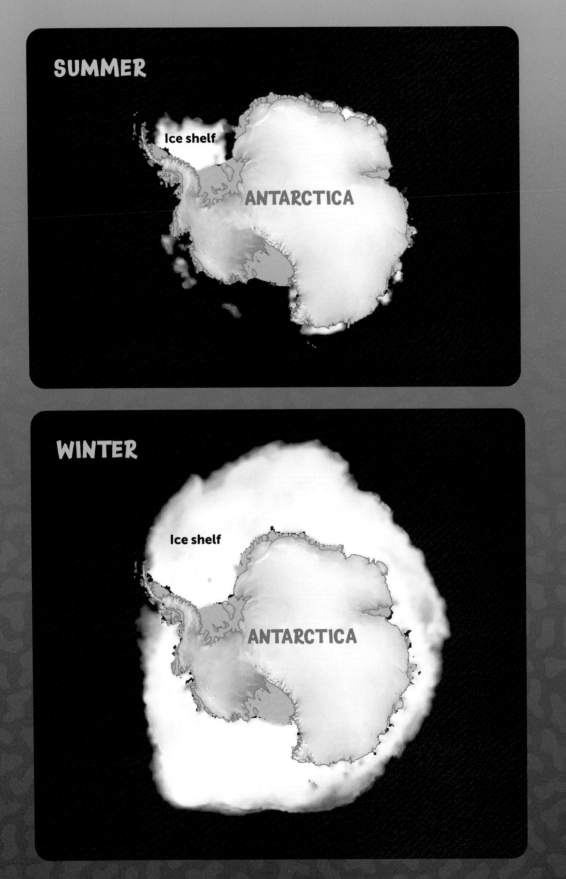

31

FUN FACTS!

Adélie penguins lack teeth. Instead, barbs on the roof of their mouths and their tongues help them grip and swallow slippery seafood.

Adélie penguin flippers are hard and so strong that flipper whacks are like wooden-paddle smacks.

Adélie penguins digest their food so quickly that they can poop about every 20 minutes.

An Adélie penguin's feather coat is key to surviving in ice-cold Antarctica. So, each year, adult Adélies go ashore and don't eat for about three weeks while shedding old feathers and growing new ones.